WHEN A BLOOMING BUD WHISPERS

THAÏNA EDMA

Copyright © 2017 Thaïna Edma

Thaïna Edma

All rights reserved.

ISBN: 1975650530
ISBN-13: 978-1975650537

DEDICATION

To you,
May you always find a reason to read beyond the lines and
remember that,
No matter how small your light may be, it still has the
mysterious power
To cast out the darkest shadows.

Ty.

CONTENTS

Budding	3
Blooming	13
Maturing	31
Wilting	47
Seeding	59
Acknowledgements	77

PAUSE

To me, the concept of changing seasons is very amusing yet somehow sacred. There's always an excitement for the upcoming change and yet a regret for the one passing – just like in our time we find joy for new adventures and new beginnings but always a sudden sadness for the moments, places, and even people left behind.

I understand it; it's an emotional attraction that keeps us glued to what we know; to our comfort zone. This is found in being human … in being a walking canvas of passed memories and influences. I realize that.

But you see, the magic of changing seasons is not a complete elimination of what was there before. On the contrary, it is a cleanse of what needs to be renewed or rebuilt.

When Fall comes around it does not destroy a whole tree, it does not uproot it from its home…not at all! It simply kisses away the dead leaves in order to make room for the birth of new and living ones from Spring's love… And so, just like the seasons, life sometimes slowly washes away parts of our canvas that aren't so pleasant in order to give way to new, amazing and beautiful art. And regardless of time, it still comes back around and washes it off, again, for the sweet whispers of blooming buds.

Thaïna Edma

Budding

WAKE ME UP WITH HONEY

You

With the mahogany glaze,

Would you sweeten my soul

By being the dab of honey

In my morning tea?

MAGICAL HOUR

I heard your smile last night,

Right at that magical hour.

It elevated my senses,

Past logic,

Past me.

For you see,

It made me see alluring and unexplainable aromas

which

Tasted like the sweetness of life,

All through the feeling of warmth

In your dome of familiarity.

So yes,

I heard your smile last night,

Right at your magical hour.

MOON

'Moon'- He breathed me as so.

Nonchalantly,

Yet explicitly glorious.

Subtle reminder

Of an entire existence

Spent kissing flawed titles.

AS I FORGOT TO CALL YOU MINE

Just like that,

Blindsided and all,

Fate stepped in,

And here you were,

Ready to play house,

with the demons

That I held…

FEED ME A KING

My Dearest drop from God,

I wonder what your skin

Tastes like in the morning;

Or if the magic of your kiss still entices

With the sunset as it does its rise.

King,

If I stripped your modest walls

With the melody of my fingers,

Would I still be able to see

Your soul sparkle this midnight?

For you see,

I crave you in your most

Undiluted,

Unconfined state.

Raw.

Do you permit?

Or should I still wonder

About the beauty of your imperfections?

THE RARE TRAIT OF GRATITUDE

Say thank you to strength

For it allows me to search

Shamelessly

After this soul that you

So beautifully hide.

VOWS

Faithfully be mine

And I promise you,

Just like Helios selfishly

Paints light onto his Selene,

I will forever make you

My virgin canvas

Onto which I pour

My love and my soul.

SCULPTING GRACE

You called out love for me,

Carved out sin from me,

Breathed life into me,

Effortlessly,

Unwittingly,

Yet gracefully,

You tamed my demons,

All while reviving my desire

To selfishly be Yours.

Blooming

THE WAR WE HAVE YET TO WAGE

Partake with me

In this sea of speculators,

Let what we birth here

Be the sign They search for.

May the elevation of the waves

Be the creator of the motions that

Will have us surpass

The doubt that They carry.

Our kill,

Let it be so swift and clean

That it becomes Their catalyst.

Keep the consistency of our devotion

And partake with me

In this sea of non-believers

And let what we gather here tonight

Be the proof that They seek.

REPETITION

Allow your thoughts

To devour my being

All while your heart

Grasps hold onto my skin.

Although your soul

Searches for my Abyss,

It encourages your words

To kiss shivers down my spine,

And your trust

To bring these lips

Into existence.

And right when your light

Reaches its peak of ecstasy,

When A Blooming Bud Whispers

Your strength finds perfumed breaths

To gently seek out this Queen.

Again.

OPENED WINDOWS & BURNING SAGE

Midnight whispers

Between these sultry sheets,

Have this savage grace waking up

At the sound of your name.

Gasp.

Release.

My oh my, do they carry You oh so beautifully…

Shameless remembrance of all things that is sweet,

Of all things that is You.

FRAGMENT PIECES

Spoil me.

Let your spilled tint

Claim the purest corner

Of this canvas that was

Once yours...

So I can revisit the sultriness

Of your bold strokes

That was once mine...

Once more...

EARNED

Every so often,

This wild world

Robs you of your gentle spirit,

The strength of you crown.

So when the Moon wildly sings,

And gives way to Her shining love,

I invite you,

My sweet, sweet King

To bring me your hunger

Your thirst and your wants,

For you will find rest

In the bosom of my Oasis.

FOREVER YOURS

For the good,

Not so good but

Never bad enough

To not be good,

Love always chose me

And I, forever, You.

BURNING CANDLES

These venomous flower petals

Dripping of gold nectar

Have you jaded for

You fight me too much Love

Give way to these nude kisses to

Ease these tender convulsions

Of me running through your veins

Or die with my name grazing your lips.

STAINED

For my fingers sometimes fail me

I now ask you

To stand back and carefully

Watch me while I politely

Undress you with my words.

HOME

I've missed moments,

Places and people before

But not the way that

I missed [YOU] last night.

[YOU]: the Home divinely built

As the sanctuary for my soul

To find rest.

CARVE MY NAME WHERE LOVE PERMITS

If you can still manage

To say my name without

The most painfully pleasurable shiver

Running through every fiber of your being,

That means my imprint wasn't deep enough

And these love marks weren't strong enough

…I still have work to do.

MORNING

Slowly,

For I ask that I be the first

Inducing thought that moves you

Over the unidentified line

Between death and life.

Allow me to be your sunrise,

With that,

No matter the turns of the day,

I vow to smear colors

Onto your gentle soul

Every sunset.

So do me a favor,

Before you charm the idea of

Waking up and dancing with the Sun,

Let me be your first

Penetrating thought.

3 AM COMPANY

For sometimes,

The world gets too big,

Too scary

And the only place I find refuge

Is with you…

In your arms…

Where I lose myself

But recover my heart.

So quiet down these words my love

And listen

To the poetry of my silence.

SPOILED LITTLE ONE

I felt and tasted your being.

Never will I be able to forget

The flavor it brought to my life,

And the appetite it bloomed in

My Soul.

You became my worst vice.

CLIPPED WINGS OF A SONGBIRD

I wish to stay,

I truly do,

But my Demons no longer feel safe

Within the confinement of your being

So leaving is far from being a want

But merely a necessity.

Maturing

CANVAS PAPILLON

'You.'

My flamboyant beauty,

My demented fool,

Let me read the raw map of your chaotic soul

While risking my being

To feel the strength of your divine nature.

Pardon my want to unzip your cover,

Speak to your causes and

Purify your walls,

All to paint 'You'

With the palette of my pleasure.

No foul intentions,

None but needed vows

To forever be

The bare inspiration

In your tangled midnight sheets

Tied to your heart,

To your truth,

To 'You'.

CRADLED DREAMS

You always reminded me of Home,

I guess that's why

Curling up within your soul

Always felt so right.

So do me justice and be

The breathless paradise

That I've always dreamed of.

JADEN MOVÉ

Let it be

Where it needs to be.

This flower,

Let it be rooted so deep in your being,

That it finds life to sing,

To breathe,

And to be.

There I will completely let go

And be where I need to be,

With you.

In the completeness

Of your being.

THE VALLEY WHERE I MET THE SUN

Today.

I was humbly reminded of

How convincing your presence was

By the strong hold

Your heart had on mine.

SINK WITH EASE, BREATHE WITH PRIDE

Make me believe,

Beyond your abilities,

That you're purposely fighting for me

Because then, drowning would feel

More like breathing in life

Than it is kissing death.

SOUPIR

Unfolded a requiem

For this shattered branch,

Tipping nibbles

Over tainted gates.

I no longer found the burst

To end my trickling off your tongue,

Like sun brushed honey:

Strictly golden and bittersweet.

WHEN A BLOOMING BUD WHISPERS

We amplified this flourishing bud

Dancing on the canvas of your words;

So for the last time and for my sake,

Just as cracking waves drip sweets

From these parted lips,

Pray my name to Heaven's ears,

To forget mercy and oblige

My muted indulgence for

The raw nectar of your blushed petals.

MOURNED HEART MOURNS HEARTS

Out of all my sleepless Beasts,

You have been my toughest cry.

To wage war against you

Is to speak grief upon my Heart.

BEES DON'T PLEAD FOR HONEY

Reason with me,

Explain to me how,

After I basked in your existence

Day in and day out,

After you left your mark

In the locus unseen,

In midnight form,

Even after I purposely

Carried you in my heart,

Coupled you with my soul,

And as your love presently

Seeps through my vessel…

After all of that,

Explain to me how

I wake up missing you?

PROTECT YOUR ART

Before your ink runs dry

And your passion flames out,

Write me out in cursive.

Boldly jointed.

Indecently lucid.

For that's how you art.

And that's how I love.

BLUE MOON

Once in a blue Moon,

Feel the beauty of things,

Unspoken, hidden, glorious things,

Ones the eyes don't permit sight to:

Fall out and risk it.

Blindfolded, trusting and all,

Risk it and dance with your Devil...

Deviant Angels are still claimed Angels,

Fewer drops from pure,

But closest ones to truth.

OH, TO BE THE MOON'S FAVORITE LULLABY

Shuffled sheets,

Moonlight kissed.

Playful thoughts

To spirited night,

She carries their crown…

No matter the distance,

This Queen's bed

Was only made for a King.

PURPLE SUGAR

Candles bleeding,

Over nude butterfly whispers,

I reason the beauty of

Your horn bred Angels.

My rightful Saviors.

Tattooing in me fading secrets,

To reify Divinity,

With the reminder of your sway

…So I wait for them to wake,

Crowning me yours to taste.

Thaïna Edma

Wilting

ARCHAIC

Running rivers past golden waves,

Murmured soft songs to remind the heart to

Never abuse the [vulnerability]

That one lets you [feel]

For that's [trust]

In its most [intimate] form.

LAWOUZÉ

And although never promised

At every draw of the Moon

And with every cradled kiss,

Aching for a dusting of your life

On this sinner's lips

I still sneak from you

Sweet intoxicating breaths

On a debt of flushed morning dew.

I MUST

Fallen and rebirthed,

I am in the process of forgetting

Your being as a whole…

A slow dismantling process,

An unwanted process,

But a process nevertheless.

I CARRY YOU WITH ME

And as if your morphine infused aura

Didn't suffice to exhume enough colors into my life,

Here walks in your absence

That spoke lively to the darkness

In which my heart found reason to overdose in its

sadness.

COME BACK HOME

You are evermore chiseled

In places that you bred from me.

Places that I can't perforate

Without your permissive brush.

Come back home

To these cold remains

Aggressively craving

Every. Drop. Of. Your. Warmth.

Come back home.

Suppress my thirst

And breathe me life.

THE SPLENDOR OF RUINS

There's nothing left

But the sheer memory of

Vain euphoric cries.

Worthless gazes and empty words.

We left a colossal version

Of what we were,

And stepped into a sea

Filled with vacant promises.

Our scars became permanent tattoos

Inflicted by each other,

To each other,

Night after night,

Our gratification redesigned.

With that, the monsters lurking

In my dark room will forever be indebted to you,

So silencing their calls would be minor,

Since they form the memory

Of your existence.

CAN I?

Can I roll over into your arms,

Forehead kisses and all,

And claim the rhythm of your heart

As my repetitive lullaby…

Even if it's just for one night?

RAISE YOUR WORDS FOR MY SAKE

ALWAYS

Fight for what is yours

ONLY

At the moment that

It is yours to fight for.

CAGED CREATURES

Vibrant and animated,

Without warning

And without fail,

They rise up

[such empty beasts]

Howling at the Moon…

So I stand.

Again.

Jaded and departed

Pleading for rest

From our midnight ritual,

With only your name to silence Them.

Thaïna Edma

Seeding

WATER THE GARDEN

And in all, BEING heartbroken

Has the pain rooted so deep that

No number of stiches can repair the damage:

It's rotten, it's poisoned…

The poetry of the scariest pain

One can feel.

PERFUMED EMBRACE

Write love onto a woman

Who immerses her truth in your aura,

Breathes passion from your touch,

For she will forever remind

Every inch of your being that

Upon collision of penetration,

A cosmic explosion

Is waiting to birth.

GOLD HONEY, GOLD

Whether you know it or not

Even after all the dust,

Scrapes and bruises,

I still look at you

Like I acquired Gold.

FLOWERS STILL BLOOM UNDER A STORM

I am meant to be

Kissed on Fall days,

Nestled with on Winter nights,

Whispered to on Spring evenings,

And divided accordingly

Under Summer stars.

PREACH YOUR TRUTH

…And when I sometimes

Lose faith, find your reason to merge

What I know of you and

What you teach me to be your truth…

UNAPOLOGETICALLY BEING WOMAN

Need I remind you

That I'm still human,

Sometimes all that I require

Are slower breaths and

Enough time to revisit

Your penmanship on my skin,

Your lingering pecks left in unidentified corners,

The sensation of your gasps

Throughout my walls dancing with

The sweet vibration of your embrace…

Ecstatic paralysis,

Sensual blues.

Just enough time to recall,

Given they're my only memory of

How you so gently loved.

HUMAN NATURE

The page sat blank for a while,

Just like the gaze bestowed on one another.

To think that this was the point of perfection made us foolish.

Foolishness isn't created but merely in our nature.

The elapsed time spent on creating this story.

This risk taken against many odds.

And the courage it took for that first step,

All seems to bundle up into worthless energy.

Disappointment is the result of our expectations meeting our reality,

But as we try to rebalance this equation,

Reality seemed to overpower our expectations.

With the semi flashes of memories,

It makes it hard to not detail out a story from each other's eyes.

As words fill this page, it still sits blank

All because the reality of our expectations

Created a disappointment that can never be truly written.

At least not with love.

THE SHADOWS YOU LEFT

Never have I been so afraid of the night

As I am now.

I guess the darkness that you fought for me

For so long won,

Because it's back

And now you're gone.

MAY I HAVE MY HEART BACK PLEASE?

I claimed it a few places.

Shared it a few times.

I left it with you,

All while it wasn't for you;

This notion of an angel wrapped gift

With vivid petals from showered graces,

Claimed from this mahogany based home, that was

never yours.

And still I know…

I left it all with you.

Loving and all.

Broken and all.

All while it wasn't for you, amour.

But only temporarily…

SUNDAY

…Like rain.

Slow drips;

Strong cleanse,

So is love.

Uprooting the pain of past sutures

And revealing the purest version of

What is left of one's canvas.

Will you paint this life with me again darling?

Or do the memories of what's left

From these failing colors satisfy?

…Dare I ask?

KINTSUGI

Ample beams of golden love

Bearing the testimony

Of this fractured one.

Hush, gentle heart.

For you've seen the hands of this pure potter;

Distressed and defaced.

Forceful and methodical.

Molding lush existence back to this shattered spirit.

Have you ever known [brokenness]

To be so sweet and sacred?

INKED

And so I promise you,

Moving forward

Every word you will ever write

Will be written with my name

Dripping from your pen.

HEARTBEAT

Rays kiss it.

This sweet pain

From the cracks.

These colors,

No longer live.

It never stops

And slowly it arises,

The black rush,

It fills it in.

And now here we stand,

Broken,

Looking at the resurrection

Of our transgressions.

It never stops.

Thaïna Edma

I NEVER KNEW THE MOON CRIED

It sung the song it should have

This road less traveled.

Stories of fallen bleeding walls,

Of this tenancy, unconsumed.

Pure and sublime

Residing in the unknown.

Spilled in the cup of the unseen.

This split road,

This restless one

Will forever be why

The taste of honey

Revives.

Oh Heaven!

Hear the last cry

That thrusted me pass the fissure

Of immortality.

TASTE YOUR OWN CROWN

Things change.

You grow.

Drastically.

And that is perfectly ok.

No permission needed

And no approval required:

Chop up some pieces,

Add some new parts,

A scoop of patience

And a pinch of uncomfortable.

Change your recipe

In order to bring

Something new to the table.

ACKNOWLEDGEMENTS

I want to take the opportunity to say thank you to those who helped me in the creation of this book; to all of those who stepped in at the right time to be my drawing board and to those who encouraged me in the process.

Kathleen Bonany, thank you for supervising and gently dusting off my words as my editor; your care for this book helped give it life.

Thank you Joshua Noom for taking my scattered ideas and creating this beautiful artwork that I now get to hold dear to my heart.

I am very thankful for my mother, Nadine Weche Edma, who believed in what my words had to say and for pushing me past my comfort zone.

And to everyone else that I've failed to mention who have been with me the last few years on this project, you reside deeply in my heart and I am grateful for your support.

Mèsi.

Made in the USA
Lexington, KY
16 November 2017